The poetry in this book is more singularly focused than any other work I have completed. The poetry still revolves around challenges of spirituality, the difficulty of relationships and utter joy associated with them as well. And though in some regard, it is not specifically just about any one person, there are much more moments that are solely surrounding one individual. That individual is the reason for the work. The story is still being written. The rose, not only surviving the harshest scenario, but thriving is what makes the rose so special and perfect. Though it does not see its roots, its petals, nor core being or stem, it becomes an obligation to tell her the story of herself. She only grows, she doesn't she her magnanimous surroundings, the impending storms and avalanches heading her way. She only knows that were the sun is, she will grow. Seeing her heart, her will, her strength to achieve and believe in herself. And that is what makes me feel great about me, that I can recognize those characteristics in her. Shower her with as much as I can give because in her strength, I become more complete. I cannot withstand the challenges for her, they are hers; however, I can whisper in her ear that she is loved, admired and desired. To all women who are mothers, sisters or daughters, you are the rose in the eyes of so many. May you share that with each other and may we continually share this with you.

Sean Fowler

Acknowledgements and credit:

I would like to thank my family and friends for their continued support through the years, I appreciate all you have done for me. And thank you Julie and Josh, I appreciate you.

I want to thank my teachers and professors at every level of education I have had, it was you that helped foster my intellect and creative mind, from St. Leo the Great Elementary School, Brother Martin High School, Xavier University of Louisiana and the University of Phoenix.

I would like to thank Amazon.com and Createspace.com for giving all authors the opportunity to express themselves and share their work with the world.

I appreciate you all and thank you from the bottom of my heart.

Front cover photography by Julie Burke, MPH, CHES
juliemburke@gmail.com

Back cover photography by Julie Burke, MPH, CHES
juliemburke@gmail.com

Front cover conversion and editing by Josh Epperson
http://joshepperson.com

Back cover conversion and editing by Josh Epperson
http://joshepperson.com

Table of content

Sometimes
Hope is all that remains
Beautiful mess
You should let her know
Finally found myself
Never
To know you will never forgive
You
Mine
No pain

A rose in winter

A rose in winter
A beauty beyond compare
Though often times around you are not
In my heart and in my mind you are always there

A rose in winter stands singularly in a field of snow
Never does she waver
And never will she go
She represents style
Represents class
Stands for what is right
And what is good
And stands for love that truly lasts

A rose in winter is stronger than a red oak
For her strength is her smile
A rose in winter is mightier than a mountain
For her depth is her beauty
A rose in winter is warmer than the sun
For her embrace is her heart

Admire the rose in winter
Forever beautiful, intelligent, powerful she will always be
But whatever the season
And for whatever the reason
She will always be a rose to me

In the meadow

As I stood in the meadow
I saw millions of beautiful flowers
I saw azaleas, chrysanthemums, violets, mistletoe and iris
I saw tulips, magnolias, bitterroots, roses, and blossoms

I found the most graceful
Of all flowers that could be viewed
But in the sea of it all
I did not see you

I knew it to be a maze
A test of sorts
And in my craze
Crawling through the garden
Staggering on the floor
I found you
And you found me too

Lilac, beautiful and true
Purple and pure
No other view
No other flower
No other meadow
Only you

And in the meadow
I saw hope

And in the meadow
I found my faith

And in this meadow
I saw my heart

And in this meadow
I found my love

Tomorrow

Tomorrow is here like so many times before
As the sun rose this morning
So did I, as best I could not to cry
I know, and have been told of this better place
That you are resting in
And truly I believe it to me so, but that does not convince my
teary eye

A door has closed
And I knew it was the final chapter
I did not want this book to ever end but since it has I am not
mad
With each wave of emotion that I encounter
I am just sad

Saddened that your touch is no more
Saddened that I will never see your smile
Saddened, that you, would bring me through my days
And I never knew how you did it in so many ways

But here I am facing tomorrow
And it will not get any easier
Not easier at all for me
I am grateful though for my memory

My memory of each and every chapter of your life that I read
Of every word you ever said
With every passing cloud and breeze I will always be
reminded you see
Of the joys between you and me

Therefore, I will always have you
With me,
In my memory

Get down on your knees to ask

Get down on your knees to ask
Get down on your knees and pray

If it matters at all
Risk your life, your soul
If it is all the matters
If it makes you whole

Get down on your knees to ask
Get down on your knees and pray

Makes you cry
Saddened by the hour
And then you laugh with all your heart
Tears you, your life and soul apart

Get down on your knees to ask
Get down on your knees and pray

Brighter than any star
Hotter than the sun
Cooler than absolute zero
Your heart has nowhere to run

As your palms touch
And your knees burn
As anxiety covers all of you
Pray away the day
Pray away the night
And just like that

Your voice is in mind
Your kiss on my cheek
I only need to pray
Never seek
While my palms are clasped
You are with me

I am down on my knees to ask
I am down on my knees to pray

Rest assured

Rest assured a friend that is always here

Across any land, across any sea

Changing the world both far and near

Helping and guiding the night and day

Encouraging so many with her style

Living life vivaciously, that's her way

Patiently loving the masses

And loved by them too

Letting no heart not be touched

Mystically infects all she knows

Everyday her smile stays no matter what

Rendering joy wherever she goes

Blue skies

Blue skies I have dreamt for you since I heard the news
That a bundle of joy was coming to change my life
Forever, my angel, the sky is your only blues
For changing my days and my nights

As you have grown
So have I
As you have developed
You have been the joy of my eye

Forever shall it be
That until eternity is here
I will love you
Protect and watch over you

The days so tremendously long
The nights painfully rough
In my heart for you
There is no tired

Only joy, only a mother's song
And as your mother
It shall always be
There is no other
Just you, my baby, and me

My first words

My first words crossed your ears

My first steps were guarded by your arms

My first cuts were cured with your tears

And my days are overlooked with your charms

When I cried your voice calmed my fears

When I was messy, you were there to wash the dirt away

When my tummy growled or ached

Thank God for you, for goodness sake

The world may give you one day

But as I praise God for the sun and the air

You are my life and I thank God mostly for you for always

being there

The sun rose just the same

The sun rose just the same
As it did before
The moon will control
Pull and tug the shore
The same as yesterday for sure
But today is different for me evermore

The clouds rolled in
And the breeze felt as I recall
The sidewalk felt mountainous
As I took myself through the day
I could not though avoid the fall

Everything about this day
Seemed as it was yesterday
To all around nothing askew
As bright and clear the day was
So much lonelier without you

I have a lifetime

I have a lifetime
To tell you how much I love you
How amazing you are
How beautiful you are
And how much you mean to me

As you go
Along your path
You have to decide
Is that the life you want

Nothing is easy
So the struggle will be there
You have to decide
If I have to argue with someone
If I have to forgive someone
If I have to love someone and be loved
Who do I want that someone to be
I know the answer already you see
And it is not me

I only get tired

I only get tired
When you say goodnight

My day begins with your voice
As angelic as a soft light
And cuts through the morning breeze
Soothes my heart and puts my soul at ease

I only get lonely
When you say good bye

Not knowing if these eyes will see you again
Is so much to bear
I can not get out of my own mind
Until I know you will be there

I only get sad
When I see you cry

The sun should be jealous of you
The moon just the same
I always feel peace when I hear your name
But your tears, I hear and see
That just cannot be

So, put your head on my shoulder
Fall asleep on either arm
I will always keep you near
And protect you from harm

Your answer....

Will you fight for me
Will you fight for me today
And not only defend but protect me in every way
If the moon were to attack me with its' light

How long will you fight for me
Will it be until eternity
Will you fight for my tears
Will you fight for my years
Will you always be there for me
I need to know and I need to see

Is fighting worth the depth of your love for me
Will you fight for my heart
Will it forever be but never have a start
Will you fight and never quit

Will you never give up on me
Is my heart and love worth any sacrifice and worth bended
knee
Will you fight through the day
Will you fight through the night
Across the heavens, the ocean and the sea
Will you never let go
I have to ask and I have to know

I will fight for you
I will fight for your heart
I will fight for your soul
To the highest mountain and deepest sea

I will defend and protect you with everything in me
I will fight with every breath
I will fight and forsake all rest
I will fight through any test
I will always fight for you
That is what love is supposed to do

I knew long before you were gone

I knew long before you were gone
Because you could never stay
Something was always calling you away
There was always the hope the something was just meant to
be
God said here is your gift
That I will take away
To see how bad you wanted that blessing to stay

It is that, in that way
The destiny and eternity lay
Will you fight for that blessing
Will you fight for that gift
Everyday

If you will
Then put aside your fear
Know and believe that The Lord loves you dear
And will never, ever lead you astray

God knew long before you and I
That he wanted it this way
The true test of sacrifice
The true test of will
The ultimate test of faith

Look at The Lord
To be together with each other
He will, then fulfill
Because he, and we wanted it that way

When I see you again
I will say what I should have said then

If you are upset,
Know your smile brightens the day

If you are depressed,
Know your laugh makes pain wash away
Frustrated with life,
Your angelic voice soothes the heart

Tired and just can't go on,
Your style and grace is so sexy and smart
And ever, if a tear must leave your eye
My arms to hold you will always be by

When I see you again

When I see you again
I will say what I should have said then

Tell me your name
Tell me do you feel the same
My heart has stopped
And will beat no more
Until I hear your voice
Through my corridor

I will not breath until
You are pressed against my chest

Those eyes
Captured my soul
My heart is the prize and you didn't try
Can your words
Be spoken tomorrow day
If so
Tell me where to go
And then beg me to stay

I broke my heart

I broke my heart
From the end to the start
It is okay you see
It was done by me

Do not worry
Do not cry
Do not be sorry
Dry your eye

It is in the pieces
That the puzzle
Can begin anew
It is in the heart ache
That I must navigate
To be without you

Moments of impact

Within my vision
There is an angel in my view
When you see me
A stranger you once knew

Moments of impact
A heart is broken
A heart is learning
A heart that cannot remember
And a heart that cannot forget

A moment of impact
Brought you to me
And a moment of impact
Took you away

When all around is familiar
With all that you see
I will depart
Since none of them is me

A moment of impact
Brought you to me
And a moment of impact
Took you away

He does not hate you
His heart is broken
And from that point of view
All words are misspoken

The relationship that once was
Is no more
As an onion
Lay sliced on the floor
The layers are there
But the problems are at the core
She just does not love you anymore

Don't, you'll ruin it

Don't, you'll ruin it

With so many words that

Need not be spoken

Promises given

That has never been broken

You need not say

What I see in your eyes

How you hold my hands

And caress my check

So do not speak

Words just won't do

Your heart says it all

I love you too

So, don't, you'll ruin it

You're wrong

You think I love you
Because my heart skipped a beat
Because my palms sometimes sweat
For places we remember
And places we forget

None are a reason
For my love for you

You think I love you
Because my knees get weak
Because my head spins
For endless nights
And days that barely begin

None are a reason
For my love for you

Love comes
From holding me
When I feel fears
Soothing my eyes
To hold back tears

There is no anxiety
And there is no pain
Your love
Silences my demons
Over and over again

Love is not my actions
Love is not my thoughts
Love is your voice
Love is your touch
Which wakes up early
Which stays up late

Love is simply just you, my soulmate

As I lay

As I lay
Your head rests on my arm
I feel your breath
Feel your warmth
Smell your charm

As I lay
Your leg splits mine
Almost becoming one
Feeling the heat
The burning of the sun

As I lay
Your breast covers my chest
I feel your heart
I sense your soul
And I can never let go

A

As you stand there

And have crossed my eye

The slightest of breeze passed by

This lifted your beautiful sundress

And exposed your thigh

And it was then

That I had to decide

To take a chance

Or just be another passerby

A risk I knew you were worth

And it was no ocean to cross

No mountain to climb

Simply cross the street

And say you are mine

B

Baby be mine

As I am in your aura

And our conversation has gone so well

There is more time to tell

I have your hands and you have my heart

Across time I would have gone

To know you from the start

Now we cross over to the next realm

And we have a mutual spell

As we embrace

I feel your beating heart

And you feel my heat

Our lips meet and began the journey

Follow my words

Follow my caress

With you I am no mess

With you in these arms

Find only safety

Peace

A time without stress

C

Casually the sundress moves from your shoulder

My shirt falls next to your feet

Your bra a distant memory

With my tee shirt

Sharing time on the loveseat

I feel the lace and they are simply in the way

Just a slight tug

And gone until the dawn of the next day

Our lips dance the night away

Perfectly placed, perfectly matched

Love has been hatched

Feeling each heartbeat

In unison, in rhythm

Hands are clasped

Feet under feet

Sweaty

Steamy

Amazing love between these sheets

Hold me close

Never let me go

Feel my sweat

Feel the heat

Feel the love cover you

As I do

D

Do you feel what I feel

As I know you from within

And feel your breath on my back

Feeling your sweat on my neck

A few hours done

And so much more to come

With each movement

With each turn

I see you in a new light

I see you in a new view

From behind your hair smells so nice

Perfect shoulder

Perfect back

Always will I be there to protect you

From any and all attack

As you now take control

Put me on my back

I am at your whim

Place me as you please

I will submit to you

In this position

I will always do

E

Elation as the sun is rising

You are in my arms

The day has passed

The night flew away

And left two lovers

To begin a new day

The memory of last night

Will remain with me

As with you

That is how love begins

And that is how love stings

Pillow talk

Wispy hair

Feeling you

Forever will I dare

Together now

While clothes are here and there

All over the floor

Let us not leave this bed

Let just make love so more

In the dark

In the dark
In the absence of light
Regardless of vision
Regardless of sight
Your voice leads the way
My heart follows too
Through a maze of souls
Which leads to you

In the dark
Never fearful
Never alone
Your voice leads the way
My heart follows too
Through a sea of tears
And my soul is home

In the dark
I see so clear
My being at ease
Your voice leads the way
My heart follows too
Through demons and angels
Which leads to you

When I see you again

When I see you again

I will say what I should have said then

If you are upset,

Know your smile brightens the day

If you are depressed,

Know your laugh makes pain wash away

Frustrated with life,

Your angelic voice soothes the heart

Tired and just can't go on,

Your style and grace is so sexy and smart

And ever, if a tear must leave your eye

My arms to hold you will always be by

He does not hate you

He does not hate you

His heart is broken

And from that point of view

All words are misspoken

The relationship that once was

Is no more

As an onion

Lay sliced on the floor

The layers are there

But the problems are at the core

She just does not love you anymore

Leads to you

My mind racing of years gone by
And still finds you
My thoughts are no more than wild dreams
And still finds you

Regardless of what I see
And it does not matter what I hear
My eyes finds your smile
My ears hear you laugh
And it all makes sense to be me and so true
Everything lead to you

The flower never sees itself bloom
It has to give its' beauty to the world to view
The harmony cannot appreciate its' melody
It has to its' heart and soul for our pleasure
You're my flower
You're my song
And nothing has or will ever measure

Just like that
It becomes so clear
Just like that
You have to be near

No more to say
No more to do
All I am leads to you

There

There is a day that you will be taken away

But not today

You will be called to a final resting place

But not today

We all lose the people we love

But not today

The most important leave

But not today

Since it is not today

I will love you everyday

It is not how we see ourselves

Or how the world sees us

It is how God sees us

Although

Although time continually moves
Time, she moves faster than regret
And this date proves
That the sequence even though it is a century away
You, just as the date, is special in every single way
Lives will be different when it comes around next time
The earth will be completely different too
So many things will have changed in manner and complexity
Although that will happen, love will still be true

On this date when it comes around again
This letter will have so much to say
That one hundred years ago
She was loved in such a wondrous way
Although the time will have passed
Hopefully she would know
That love was forever and did last
How amazing for the new eyes to view, and this letter will
prove and show

And that day, when it comes again
He reads this letter about his love
And compares her to you
So that she knows how special you were
So that she knows how special she is
So the world will know that even after the sun fades
Love still grows in the shades

Sometimes

Sometimes you need to go where you've never been

To see what you've never seen

To hear what you've never heard

To think what you've never thought

To smell what you've never smelled

To touch what you've never felt

To taste what you've never tasted

Sometimes you have to go where you've never been

To see where you are

So, go, you'll be fine

So, go, once, at least this time

Hope is all that remains

Hope is all that remains
And sometimes that is all that is left
And some days
The pain is indescribable
And it sits on a sorrowful heart
Pain never goes
It never sways
The pain reminds how much you are in love
And just stays and stays

But hope always remains
As the heart still beats
And refuses to rest
With the promise of a new day
With the promise of a new test

And then
You see that hope is all that you have
But that hope is enough

Beautiful mess

Such a beautiful mess
I see beyond the exterior
And pass by each layer
Viewing your beauty
And viewing your soul
With an amazing inner glow
Such a beautiful mess

Beneath I do see so clearly
With a graze here
To wash your cheeks
And a graze there
Getting the mess from your hair
You start to show what the world sees
It is what I already know
Such a beautiful mess

Yes, you are a mess
And how did it come to be
Your mess is no more
Your mess is no less
Than the mess that is me

I will clean brow, wash your face
I will clean your arms, wash your hair
I will clean and wash you everywhere

While I do
Tell my dear what happened to you
How did you get to be in distress

How did you become such a mess

And as you tell your tale
I will listen with open arms
To protect you from the world
To protect you from harm

And though a mess you may be
And a mess you become again
I will always have an open heart
I will always have open arms
For you to rest in
I must confess
I do love
Such a beautiful mess

You should let her know

You should let her know

Saying what needs to be said
So that she never lets go
If you love her
Do not allow her to guess
Do not make her insecure
She cannot read your mind
Show her your heart is pure

You should let her know

Listening when you want to speak
So she will never let go
Do not just hear
Listen to her concern
Listen to her fears
She wants to give you herself
In every way
You might miss her pain
If you close your ears

You should let her know

Holding her side
So she will never let go
Hug her being
Wrap your arm around her soul
Grasp what protection feels like
Strength in the freedom

To conquer the world
And a secure place to rest
Give her that security
Give her your all

You should let her know
So that she never lets go
Tell her;
Listen to her
Hug her

You should let her know
That you will never let go

Finally found myself

Finally found myself
Not knowing
Through all encountered
That I couldn't be anyone else

Looking in to my eyes
As deep as my vision allows
As far as my heart goes
Past my being
To finally see my soul

Finally found myself
Not knowing what would be there
Not knowing when it became to be

Finally found myself
Not knowing how I did not see
Not knowing why I did not know

That the fire that burns so bright
That fire deep within me
That fire that drives my thoughts
In the morning and the night
Leads me
Guides me
Shows me

I always knew the way
Too afraid to move
And too afraid to stay

Finally found myself
Was not where I thought
Not where I looked
Not where I sought
I was never here
Nor there

Until I found you
I understand now
That I am everywhere

I finally found myself
It is with you
And nowhere else

Need to write
"I can see you in a crowd
everyone is faceless when you're around "

Never

I never should have let you go
So much I could not say
And even more
So much I could not show

And I see now
It was more to do with me
And less to do with you
As strong as I am now
I was then too
I just, until now, never knew

I never should have let you go
So much I could not say
And even more
So much I could not show

You are not as distant as the stars
And I see them in your eyes
As close as can be
So close to see your touch
Closer to hear your breath
So close to feel your heart
Against my chest

I never should have let you go
So much I just did not know
And how to get you back
And where can I stand
Keeping both hearts intact

Loving as time does demand

I never should have let you go
And now I do see
As the sun does shine
As the wind does blow
As the earth does turn
What matters is so clear
What concerns me so near

It is each day I am awake
It is your voice
It is your presence
That lives within me

To know you will never forgive

That you will never forget

In order to live

I have the regret

Hurting you is not my wish

And I would take it away

If only I could

The line though has been drawn

Nothing now can ever come to any good

Saddened that the end is near

And the future unclear

You

I saw this woman
I told her she was beautiful
Lovely
Amazing
Statuesque, a vision to view
I could not help myself
I had to stare
But she was not you

I met a lady
We talked
She was brilliant
I love how we communicate
About life
About love
Chemistry
Oh, Algebra too
A dork, I am, maybe
A nerd, yeah, me, indeed
But she was not you

An apparition appeared
I see your heart
Can cure your ills
Love you
To the end
From the beginning
Am wondrous
All I meet would concur
I see your soul

I too see though, I am not her

She, her, them
A room of all
I could know
I could view
And I stand in the crowd
All would know
They have no chance
For my heart
And my love belong
To you

Mine

The moon is yours
If you want it
Simply say so
And off will I go
And then it will be there
Laying at your feet
At your door

And you say, are you mine?

A walk on the beach
With your hand in mine
Watching the waves
Crash here
Crash there
Being broken by the rocks
And none compare
To the strength I feel
When I am on my knees at your feet

And you say, are you mine?

When I hold you
Around your waist
I feel you breath
When you inhale
When you exhale
As I hold you close
Next to my chest
I hear you heart

Each beat
A pair, indeed we are, never apart

And you say, are you mine?

I chose you
Over and over again
And the answer
To your question
Are you mine?
Yes, I am
Every time
Every time
Every time

No pain

When she is said
When she feels alone
When she is mad
When she wants to stay home
And when she feels life is a drain
Though that hurts me more

I will see her through
For her I feel no pain

Though she is tired
Though she thinks at times she is a mess
Though she is pulled and stretched
And though everyday another test
And when she feels life is a strain

I will see her through
For her I feel no pain

I am the lucky one
I know her heart
I love her eyes
And I love her hair
I cherish her time
Enamored by her stare
I see behind her eyes
To the depth of her soul
And it is there
I will go again and again

No pain
No pain

I will carry her
Again and again
For her all my love
For me no pain no pain

She is my breath
Again and again
For her all my love
For me no pain no pain

Made in the USA
Charleston, SC
22 April 2015